Stories from around the Globe

the Globe

Volume Three

Sharon Brown

(MO2VATE Media)

Published by The Book Chief Publishing House 2022
(a trademark under Lydian Group Ltd)
Suite 2A, Blackthorn House, St Paul's Square,
Birmingham, B3 1RL
www.thebookchief.com

British Library Cataloging in Publication Date: A catalogue record
for this book is available from the British Library.

Book Cover Design: Deearo Marketing
Editing / Typesetting / Publishing: Sharon Brown

THE BOOK CHIEF®
IGNITE YOUR WRITING

Table of Contents

Dedication

To all of the amazing women all over the world who are fighting some incredible battles and pushing through the toughest of challenges to create a life they love.

Foreword

By Jackie Frith

I had a dream of becoming a published author for quite some time but always thought it would be one of those dreams that never actually happen or come true, until I discovered mo2vate magazine this year, this is when things changed quite a lot for me on the writing front.

When I saw they were asking for women who had an inspiring story to tell for the March 2022 edition of the magazine it piqued my interest somewhat. I didn't do anything about it at first as I told myself that as my story is of a spiritual nature, then it wouldn't really fit in with the theme of the magazine as I assumed it was just for business articles. When I asked the question about if my story would be suitable and I was given a resounding yes, I decided now was the time to go for it.

I felt so much pride when it was accepted by the editor, that I jumped at the chance to become a featured author in this book as I was more confident about expanding on my inspirational message to reach more people and of course have the opportunity to call myself a published author.

For the April edition of the magazine I decided to step right outside of my comfort zone and write a business article about how important it is to know who your ideal clients are. I had only moved over into the business coach arena the year before and actually didn't think I was really qualified to be able to give my opinion or thoughts on these topics, so you can imagine my surprise and delight when I was told that they liked my article that much that they were featuring it as a centre spread.

If you have ever had a dream of writing articles and books but have done nothing about it then take this as your motivation to make it happen because one day you could be writing the forward for a book that you have written a chapter in just like me.

Take inspiration from the stories you will read over the coming pages and start the ball rolling by making that first contact with Mo2vate magazine, as you never know where it might lead you too and what doors it will open. This is a great quote by Stephen Covey and is so very true, make the right decisions and your life and business will fly.

"I am not a product of my circumstances. I am a product of my decisions." — Stephen R. Covey

Introduction

This book is a real mix of inspirational stories from adversity to triumph and real-life adventures that some can only dream of.

Each woman has highlighted specific times in their lives and documented their memories to take you the reader on a journey.

It's a difficult thing to do when you open yourself up to anyone and by sharing their stories in this book, these inspirational ladies have stepped out of their comfort zones in the hope they can inspire someone else.

HILARY THOMSON

HILARYTHOMSON.COM

Chapter 1

Lesson from Snowdonia

By Hilary Thomson

I could feel the sweat trickle down my back; my breath caught in my throat. I put one foot in front of the other, wiped my brow and adjusted my laden backpack so the straps would stop cutting into my shoulder.

My calves were crying out.

I was hot.

I had too many clothes on.

I lifted my head to look up and saw a line of backpacks disappearing in the distance. I was falling behind.

We had been walking for ten minutes when I saw a group of people sitting down on the side of the track, taking a break, their voices carrying in the wind as they laughed and joked.

My legs were sore.

We had only just started.

I had another seven hours.

What had made a fifty-five-year-old woman decide to climb Snowdonia on a whim?

It started in a Facebook Group where I replied to someone looking for an extra person to climb Snowdonia as part of a charity climb.

I had heard of Snowdonia. It was a mountain range. It was supposed to be pretty. The views would be amazing. It was spring, and it looked like good weather.

My favourite memory was trekking in Nepal in my youth. I climbed Mt Kenya when I was age eighteen and had always wanted to do more climbing and trekking. I liked walking and was always up for a challenge, so I put my hand up to say I was interested, not thinking much of it. I got a notification that night to say I was in and to make my way to Wales. The climb was in two days.

It was all paid for, and all I had to do was get to the destination. We would climb late in the day and reach the peak for sunset. How hard could it be? I enjoyed walking; I was pretty fit.

Okay, maybe not as fit as I used to be but surely, it's just a long walk. How wrong I was!

I drove over five hours from London to the Welsh village of Llanberis, North Wales. The hotel was in a small town at the bottom of the mountain range. I was meeting strangers. I had never met these people. I had butterflies.

What if I didn't like them? I knew nothing about them. I met them in the hotel bar, the group consisted of two work colleagues and I was replacing the third work colleague who couldn't make it. We chatted for a while, had a quick drink and decided to go to a restaurant that evening to get to know each other. It was an evening of shared experiences and laughter and I knew I had made the right decision. It was a pleasant evening, and by the time we retired, I was excited about the climb ahead and glad I had taken the chance to say yes.

I didn't sleep a wink that night. Strange bed and strange surroundings. It's funny how quiet the countryside is.

I am used to the hustle and bustle of the city, with the lights and sounds of cars and people. The bed was uncomfortable, and a fan somewhere was whirring all night.

Bleary-eyed, I made my way to breakfast, not in the mood for a chat or small talk and a bit grumpy. It was going to be a long day.

We explored the town, rested in the afternoon and prepared our provisions for the climb.

We were briefed on being prepared for any eventuality as the weather could turn on the ascent, so my backpack was laden with extra water, waterproofs, a first aid kit, and protein bars. It was heavy. It turned out to be a lovely afternoon, with no wind and warm sunshine, and it looked like it was going to stay that way on the climb.

We assembled at the meeting point at 4 pm with a group of twelve people ranging from 18 to 65 years old. I didn't feel so bad at that point.

As people gathered, I began to get excited about the climb, eager to see the beauty of the landscape, keen to get moving, and excited about the challenge. This was an area I had never been to, and the memories of my climb up Mt. Kenya came flooding back, albeit without the bone-numbing cold, icy blasts and altitude sickness that I experienced there, where it can get down to below -30c.

Here I was in the middle of England, climbing a mountain range and comparing it to Mt. Kenya; it couldn't have been more different.

We set off, walking in a line, slowly at first. I was up at the front for all five minutes. We turned down a side road and started the ascent up a tarmac road. To say it was steep is an understatement. After two minutes, I was out of breath and tried to pretend all was okay, silently crying inside, wondering why I had decided to put myself forward for this. Doubts crept in the further I walked.

One by one, each of the group passed me, chatting and laughing without a care in the world. I couldn't even talk; I was so out of breath.

My calves began to scream; I reached for my water bottle; I needed to stop, but I couldn't. We had only just set off. Everyone was forging forward. I felt old, inadequate, and like giving up, and we had only just started.

I was now the last in the line. I was falling behind.

I could almost feel the eyes on me, pitying me, wondering why this old lady had even bothered and as their eyes rested on me, I knew they were hoping they would not be asked to wait for me or help me along.

I put one foot in front of the other, and slowly but surely, I reached where everyone had gathered for a rest. No sooner had I plonked myself down than everybody started to get up and walk again.

Noooooo, my body screamed; I had only just gotten here. I powered down some water and a protein bar, got my breath back, stood up and continued the climb.

It was a steadily ascending path and as I looked into the distance, I could see the line of people in our group snaking their way upwards.

They seemed a long way off. I tried not to think of how far away they were.

I was determined to get to the summit by sunset. Stopping or quitting was not an option for me. I would need to dig deep. I decided to enjoy the scenery and look up rather than focus on my feet.

The ascent was gentle, although I was very often out of breath. I stopped often. It was a path full of pebbles, so you had to be careful where you put your foot. My group went on ahead.

One of the things I did when the going got tough was to focus on a point some way ahead of me, made it a focal point and focused on that point.

By focusing on the small goals, I gained more traction, which made the ascent more achievable as I kept focusing on the next small goal. I didn't let my mind wander.

We had a guide by my side the whole time walking with me and distracting me with his conversation. I wouldn't let my mind go to where I knew it would be easy to go…to decide to stop and go back down. I focused on a stone ahead, the scenery, or conversing with the guide.

After we had been walking for about two hours, I started to flag again and had to dig deep to keep moving forward.

I had a secret up my sleeve for when things got tough. I have a mindfulness activity which is simple and effective. It involves rubbing my two fingers together, feeling the ridges on the skin and the temperature, and focusing on my breathing in and out. While I focused on this, I kept putting one foot in front of the other. It took my mind off the pain of walking, and I could switch to the feeling of my fingers on my hands, which created the distraction I needed.

It sounds like a pretty easy thing to do, but it's effective. I carried on doing that as I climbed. There were times when I was so out of breath I could hardly breathe and had to stop, but I kept telling myself to go at my own pace. I ignored everyone who was up ahead and focused on myself and my journey. It didn't matter how quickly I got to the summit; I knew I would get there, it didn't matter how fast. It was my journey and no one else's.

As we neared the summit, we could hear the cheers of the others further ahead; I kept telling myself it was only around the next corner. That kept me going.

I finally turned the corner and saw the group all sitting down, enjoying the view, some even having a cup of tea. I breathed a sigh of relief, and a huge smile crept onto my face, my first in a while. We had made it for the sunset.

What a view. As the sun went down and I caught my breath, I reflected on how a lot of what I had been through to get to the summit is what entrepreneurs, me included, go through in our entrepreneurial journey.

The thoughts and feelings we go through as entrepreneurs are a rollercoaster of emotions and sometimes result in a lack of motivation and momentum.

There are days when you are enjoying the journey, you feel on top of the world, and yet there are days when it is hard, you feel like you are walking through treacle or up a mountain, and you find it hard to keep going.

Snowdonia reminded me of my journey through entrepreneurship. How you get excited at the beginning of the journey, and then as you grow, there are difficult times when you have to dig deep to keep going.

The secret sauce is to get focused and have unequivocal self-belief that you will make it to the top.

I can't count how often I have compared myself to others who may be younger, fitter or more knowledgeable instead of looking at my journey as mine and mine alone.

Not being afraid to stop and stand back to see what we can do better.

Staying motivated on the journey when things don't move as quickly or go our way. Failing sometimes and picking yourself up to try again. Celebrating our wins, however small and looking at how far we've come. Not being afraid to dig deep and do what works for you. Keep up the momentum no matter what happens, and keep going.

Having the guide with us was invaluable; a bit like a coach, someone to keep you accountable, cheer you on, act as a sounding board, someone who helps you see how far you've come.

Back to that mountain, as the sun was setting and it was getting dark, we had to get back down the mountain range. The thought was daunting. We set off down the mountain. A quarter of the way down, we had to traverse a mountain pass, a small strip of land with a steep drop below. The wind had picked up, and 50-mile-hour winds whirred in our ears and pulled back our cheeks as we tried to get around the pass. At one point, I got down on my knees and crawled to make it to the other side. I have never been so scared in my life.

The wind was howling around our ears, and we could hardly see our next step at one point. It took all of fifteen minutes to make it across the pass but it felt like a lifetime.

It was a slow and steady walk down the mountain, clear and cold, as we walked by the light of the moon. Ultimately, we were the final descendants off the mountain and arrived at midnight. I had made it, sore and exhausted, back down the mountain. I had not let the thought of giving up enter my mind. I was going to make it.

If I could do this, I could do anything. It ignited my resolve to keep moving forwards and say yes to things I was afraid of.

It was an incredible experience and one I will never forget.

When the going gets tough in my business journey, I think back to my Snowdonia climb.

Snowdonia taught me that you can do whatever you want to do, have the courage to do the thing that scares you the most, make a plan, take one step at a time, keep in your lane, stop when you need to, ask for help and above all keep going because the rewards on the other side are priceless.

You are never too old; you have a life to live; grab it with both hands and forge ahead.

Never too old; life is short; take those chances, dare to say yes to a challenge, dig deep when the going gets tough and know that whatever you experience, this will pass. It will not last forever, and you will have stories and experiences to recount.

Have the courage to permit yourself to step outside your comfort zone, to feel the fear and do it anyway. Your life will be richer because of it.

I slept well that night. Now, where is my next adventure?

JACKIE FRITH

JACKIEFRITH.COM

Chapter 2

From Non-Believer to Teacher

By Jackie Frith

Hello, I'm Jackie, and I want to share my journey and how I got from being a complete Non-Believer to a Teacher.

Before my transformational journey started, I wasn't spiritual in any way, shape or form; I didn't believe in anything. My sister was very much into angels and had tarot readings, and I remember thinking, oh no, that's not for me; it's way too spooky and just not appealing.

Whenever she spoke to me about it, I would roll my eyes and dismiss it as I had zero interest in any of it, and if I'm honest, I thought it was a load of rubbish.

However, when I think back, I do remember when I moved into my house, which would have been a few years before I started on my spiritual journey, I woke up in the early hours of the morning, and there was a woman in nightwear standing at the bottom of my bed. I was like, OMG, who is this? I pulled the covers over my head and then looked again, and she was still there; I closed my eyes and opened them again, and she was still standing there. Honestly, I didn't know what to think as I had never experienced anything like this before and still, to this day, I don't know who this woman was, but then I just forgot all about it until the day my life changed completely.

Before my Spiritual Awakening, as I like to call it, happened, I recall that every night when I closed my eyes, there would be faces appearing in front of my face; this was scary, and I didn't know how to make it stop, and I never told anyone as I thought that people would think I was either mad or mentally ill, so I kept it to myself.

It wasn't until I started to understand more about our 6th sense that I realised this was part of being Clairvoyant - which means clear seeing - and it was spirits who were trying to contact me - and I learnt how to control it and to stop it from happening as frequently, I still get them occasionally now, but I tell them to go away and leave me alone which usually works.

Let's go to the day when the life I knew started to unravel and change in a direction I never thought possible for a Non-Believer. In May 2004, I was driving to my sister's in Carlisle, and I had a new car that I'd not had very long and loved a metallic blue Peugeot 207. I remember setting off from work in Sheffield and driving on the parkway to get onto the Motorway, and I kept getting the word accident in my head repeatedly. I dismissed it as I didn't understand what it meant, but I was soon going to find out.

I was driving in the fast lane of the M6 at around 70 miles an hour, and I lost control of the car and ended up spinning across the whole carriageway of the motorway and landed in a ditch. It all happened so fast, but I remember thinking oh, this can't be happening, please somebody help me!

When the car stopped spinning, I realised that, thankfully, I wasn't hurt and no other vehicles had been involved, but a couple of cars had stopped and were

—

shouting at me to get out of the vehicle; the exhaust pipe was sticking out of the front of the car, and I think they thought it might catch fire.

The police said that I had two blow-outs which seemed highly unusual. Still, there was no other explanation as to what had happened but bearing in mind this was a busy Friday night on the M6, I was lucky to be alive or at last not seriously hurt, unlike my lovely car, which unfortunately was written off.

If you've ever been in a car accident, you will know how scary it is and how it affects you emotionally. To this day, 18 years later, I still feel the emotion bubble up when I think about that day or drive past where it happened.

This was the start of a turning point in my life because it made me then think somebody or something was looking out for me that day because what are the chances of having an accident on a very busy motorway on a Friday night, and for me to be able to walk away unhurt and no other cars involved.

After that day, I split up with my "then" boyfriend and spiralled into a deep depression and used alcohol as my crutch to block out the emotions and to help me sleep, don't get me wrong, I wasn't an alcoholic, but I did have an alcohol dependency, I used to get through the day by dreaming about the bottle of wine I would drink when I got home. It's hard to pinpoint exactly what triggered the depression; I think it's something I've always been prone to have throughout my life,

I had an excellent job, a very good salary managing American Express, a lovely house, and a nice car, but it just always felt as if something was missing in my life, but I couldn't figure out what it was.

I worked with a very spiritual girl, and she said she knew someone who might be able to help me and asked for a piece of my jewellery so that her friend could tune in and see what she could pick up. I thought it was a load of codswallop, but I still gave her a ring to pass on. The week after, she returned the ring and started reeling off all the things her friend had said about me, which were true.

I couldn't comprehend how she could get all this information from a ring?! This is known in the spiritual world as psychometry, but at the time, I had never heard of it, and I just thought, wow! If she could get this from a ring, what could she get if I saw her face to face?

I agreed to go and see her, and after I had made the appointment, my colleague said, just to let you know, she's a white witch! What….oh dear, what was I getting myself into? I wondered, as this was so far out of my comfort zone that it made me feel sick just thinking about it.

The day of my appointment arrived, and as I was driving to see her, I was crying in the car because I felt so desperate, lonely, and so out of sync with everything, and it felt like my life was falling apart.

She answered the door dressed all in long white flowing clothes and a lovely smile; I instantly felt calm in her presence. We talked in the kitchen while she made a drink, and she told me how she had manifested her dog; at that point, I nearly got up and left as my reaction was you can't manifest a dog, you either have one or you don't. Little did I know that this was the start of my journey into learning all about manifesting and the Law of Attraction.

We sat down in the lounge for my session, and she asked me to hold my hand out, and she started reading my palm; the first thing she said was, "ooh you're highly psychic; if you wanted to read Tarot cards, you could" I had no desire to read Tarot cards or any other type of card for that matter. She carried on and said, "you're very spiritual, highly spiritual" of course, I denied it as I didn't like anything to do with church or angels or whatever else came into the "spiritual" bracket.

Then came her pièce de résistance, "you're a victim of your thoughts" Huh! How rude, I had just met this woman, and she was telling me all this stuff that I didn't like. She said, "you bring about what you think about, so when you're thinking negatively, that's when negative things happen in your life." Woah, I felt as if I had just been slapped across the face as this struck a nerve.

She sent me on my way after the session with a book to read, of which I can't remember the name, but I know

---

from that moment my life changed completely. This is where my spiritual journey began.

I became interested in angels and working with the Angelic Kingdom daily by talking to them and asking for guidance.

I stumbled across the Law of attraction as I was researching positive thoughts, my interest peaked, and I resonated with it so much that I just devoured everything I Could read about it.

By 2006 my whole life was focused on discovering more about Spirituality and the Law of Attraction. This was when I left American Express and the well-paid job and set up as a travel agent working from home. That year I also became attuned to Reiki level one and level two, along with Indian head massage.

I started to have reiki and massage clients, and in 2011 I set up my holistic practice, where I offered healing sessions, massage and other therapies.

Joining a psychic development group was the next thing I did and again was a huge learning curve and inspiration for me. When I went to the first class, I was so nervous and felt utterly useless as I couldn't get any messages from people, read cards, jewellery or see people's auras as the other students could. It felt alien to me, but I loved it. When driving home, I felt so emotional because I felt like I had found what I was looking for and that I wanted to carry on this path of developing my psychic abilities and spiritual learning. I kept going to the classes, and it still took me a couple of years to notice that I was psychic and could read people and their situations and what may happen to them in the future - not everything but some important things.

There is a misconception that people assume being psychic means you are a fortune teller or clairvoyant when these are entirely different things. We have moved on quite a lot from the velvet dresses, black table cloths and crystal balls that people often associate with psychics. Being clairvoyant means "clear-seeing", where images are usually given during readings or when the spirit shows itself to you - not reading someone's mind or giving future predictions.

All these years later, I am still obsessed with everything spiritual and still feel like I have lots more to learn, as I believe we are always on a journey of self-development.

I now teach people how to develop this side of them, and I also can empathise with those who feel like I did all those years ago because I believe we all have this ability.

Still, it often just lies dormant in people until the time comes when it needs to open and be trained, just like any other skill we would want to learn. Of course, not everyone is destined on the path of being psychic or spiritual, and I certainly didn't think that I would be far from it. Still, here we are 18 years later, and I can honestly say it's the best thing that has ever happened to me. I wish I had embarked upon my spiritual path sooner, but equally, I know that these things are planned out well before we come to earth in the human body and that we develop when the time is right for us.

My teaching role started after I became a Reiki Master in 2013, which allowed me to teach and attune people to the Reiki healing modality; from there, I branched out into teaching angel card workshops and Law of Attraction workshops which I loved doing. I knew this was the missing piece of my life puzzle.

During lockdown, I had another career-changing move as my travel business was wiped out overnight due to flights being grounded. I realised this was the time for me to focus on my spiritual business of teaching, which is where my real passion was. I became a Spiritual Life Coach, which again was another turning point for me and helped me to map out what I wanted to do with the rest of my life and who I could help with my newfound skills and qualification that I had gained.

I had a Spiritual Facebook group and found that a lot of people were asking for help in terms of their business and getting it up and running, these questions were especially coming from students who I had taught Reiki to, and it spurred me into another entirely different direction of helping Spiritual female business owners to create a life and business that aligned with their Soul purpose and passions.

They are taught how to do the treatments and read cards or teach courses, but they aren't shown how to set up the basics of being in business and creating content that speaks to their Ideal Clients, so I decided that I would make a membership just for this. I love my work and feel highly fulfilled in it. This hasn't come without its challenges, as the imposter syndrome has shone its light many times for me as I embarked on becoming a business coach and completely changing my business. I would ask myself, "Who am I to teach people how to run a business?" "Why would people pay me to teach them about business things?" "I don't earn six figures, so surely I shouldn't be a coach" "Noone will listen to me, or they will think, who is she to do this?"

All these thoughts have held me back on my journey because I have questioned if this is the right path for me so many times, but as a mentor once said to me, if people ask you questions about something, then you can teach it. You only have to be a few steps ahead of the people you lead.

I love my members and the feedback I get from them, which has to be enough to know that I am helping people create something worthwhile. I am worthy of teaching them what I know and have learnt over the 36 years of my career, as many of my skills from managing staff are very much transferable into being a business coach.

I now know that this is my life and soul purpose, and I cannot wait to see where this new journey takes me and how many more people I can help on the way.

When we embark on our spiritual path, it isn't always easy and laid out in front of us like some people seem to think it will be, which for a control freak like me can be very daunting but what I have learnt is that often we have to go with the flow and not try to force things to work because that's when resistance can hit. We end up pushing upstream instead of flowing.

When we lose the need to control every little thing in our lives and concentrate on doing what lights us up and makes us happy, then things will start to flow to you and opportunities you never thought possible will open up.

JACQUELINE KENT

JACQUELINEKENT.CO.UK

Chapter 3

The Dawn of a Brand New Day

By Jacqueline Kent

Life would never be the same again – and I was so thankful for that. At 41 years old, my marriage of 13 years was over, but I felt so calm about it all – excited even!

I drove my boys to the park, a little further away than our local that morning, to a park I wasn't familiar with; I was beaming with anticipation for our beautiful new life. It had taken guts to get me here; it had taken a lot of time and patience, but I knew it was the right decision in my heart. The decision to go somewhere different on this day was a fully conscious one because I knew that if you always make the same choices, nothing can ever truly change, and this has been the story of my life so far.

Let me fill you in a bit...
I'd had no idea how to break free from my abusive relationship for the longest time.

—

A toxic situation that almost saw the end of my life a little under two years before, but this time I was ready. I'd already begun the work by now, you see. I'd had way too many light bulb moments, and this time I was prepared for change – for good. I'd begun working with a life coach who made me aware of one simple fact. 'If you learn to put yourself higher up the list, everything else will fall into place'.

It sounded like total gobbledegook to me at the time; I couldn't grasp the concept, but I had paid her to help me, so it would be pretty silly not to follow her guidance. Her words were guided by doing 'the inner work', and thank goodness I listened! I could see how it seemed to other people (maybe, or was that just the negative nellies in my head?) – my two youngest sons were barely able to be left in the same room, and here I was making a plan to 'put myself first'. Well, wouldn't anyone struggle with that concept – initially?

By this time, I had already tried everything else – I'd had relationship counselling with my then-husband, we had social services breathing down our necks, we weren't even living together after over a decade of marriage, and everything felt like one big hot mess. Life was complicated, exhausting and felt damned unfair, so I was willing to try just about anything! And why couldn't it be about me instead of focusing on everyone else? I was barely holding it together. Life as a single mum (living alone, but married and working on it, man, that messes with your head!) had knocked the stuffing out of me, so I was pretty much set to be no use to anyone soon enough!

A carer for my son, 19 at the time; he has Aspergers – a form of autism - and everything revolved around his needs for as long as I can remember, and mum to my ten-year-old as well as an older son who lived in his place, I didn't feel I was much use to any of them!

The coach had been an angel sent to me to help me see how I could turn things around. And turn things around, I did. It was a matter of just a couple of months before the trip to the park mentioned above, things were resolving themselves (with little focus from me!), and life was already feeling so much easier. But that sense of relief I felt, the conversation had gone, 'so that's it then, we're done?'. 'I think we are, yes'.

———

Suppose you've ever lived with a master manipulator. In that case, you will know how hard it can be to say or express what you truly feel, and this had been my reality for too long, so to be able to 'be' in my power and be truthful – firstly with myself, and secondly to say out loud 'I'm done', without fear of the consequences was so empowering. I felt as if I was high on drugs from the euphoria of just being ready to let it all go, trusting it was the right thing.

Life got pretty good after that. I finally made choices that served my best interests without feeling like I 'had' to put his first. To some, that may sound selfish, but I'd gotten so used to putting others' thoughts and feelings before my own that it had become my normal.

When you're a mum, this is often the case, we lose our identity behind the wants and needs of our offspring, and it can be tough to find our way back. But as a partner, a wife, this shouldn't be the case. It should be equal – shouldn't it? And so, in October 2016, my journey to 'finding me' began in earnest. I no longer felt the need to justify my choices, especially when I wanted to do something that pleased me.

—

That Christmas, I joined a luxury gym with a spa, sauna, you name it, as an indulgence for the 'me' time experienced when my youngest spent weekends with his dad – and I also made full use of the facilities. I was invested 100% in getting back on track, getting to know who I was, what I wanted, and what I enjoyed – and I knew there was no way I was going to consider involving another person (okay, a man!) in this until I felt ready again.

I'd recognised from previous choices (an 11-year relationship that preceded my marriage) a relationship in which I struggled to find my voice, even though we had many happy times, including the birth of my older sons. As a result, I was very young and did not know what I wanted from the world even then!) that not giving myself any space between the two had led me down the 'people pleasing' path, which kept me in the space of never wanting to offend or upset anyone with choices that didn't match theirs!

The people-pleasing thing has long been a problem of mine – I see that now. But as things change and I evolve as a person (every day, new and wonderful things come to light), it is easier to understand how that doesn't truly serve anyone. In telling people what we think they want to hear, we deny them and ourselves simultaneously! We deny ourselves because we are not honest about what we want, and we deny them because they are not in touch with the correct version of us, who is even more magnificent than we dare to let on! Lecture over.

2016 and 2017 were life-changing for me. 2016 was the year I took back my power and finally said no to things destroying me slowly from the inside out. 2017 was even more beautiful as I stepped into that power, and my spiritual transformation began.

I signed up for distance reiki healing – sessions delivered by the woman who was sent to me on this life-changing journey. Her name is Cassandra Welford; she has been my mentor and is now my colleague and friend. Life can be amazing to you when you are open to it.

During the first half of 2017, I was throwing myself into choosing things that made me feel good every day – a choice I recommend wholly and fully to everyone I meet!

As I experienced more of this healing, it began to feel as though I walked around surrounded by an invisible force field in which all negativity bounced straight off, and I bloody loved it. For too long, my emotions had been manipulated by negative energy and poor choices, and it was only as I experienced the life-changing magic of reiki energy that I could understand how I had another option. Life was there to be enjoyed, and I was damn well going to enjoy it!

Friends and family were fascinated to see how I changed – to some, I am sure, it seemed almost an overnight transformation, but those who knew and understood the heartache and trauma beneath it all were loving and supportive of my choices as I took on a new aura of 'being'.

It was in May 2017 that I began thinking about how I would love to share this version of me with someone who deserved her. I was ready to let my hair down in my child-free time, and although I fully appreciated that I was worth the love of a good man, I began to dabble in dating apps to see if anyone took my fancy, just for something casual. I dipped my toe in once or twice, but as I was

49

only looking for something light-hearted, it would take a thunderbolt to draw my attention to anything else.

By this point, I was so full of love for myself that I wasn't prepared to be made to feel 'less than – not by anyone! I swiped right a few times with no response, but I saw one guy called Bruce who looked exactly what I was after (sounds like I was browsing a menu, doesn't it?) – no topless poses, no photos of his latest 'catch' (I'm talking fish here), just fun, entertaining light-hearted banter.

One of the things I have yet to mention about myself is I need to improve at starting conversations; I cannot make small talk! So that was what I led my profile with – contact me first if we match. And on 17/7/17, our worlds collided.

That was my thunderbolt!

I've tried to explain so many times how it felt after just one or two sentences exchanged between us, and if it's never happened to you, it might sound incredibly twee, but it's the truth. I felt these energy shivers all over; it was like someone was tickling me with electricity!

Our chatter flowed fast all day, and he asked me for a date by the end of that first day! To anyone who knew either of us at that time – we both had extensive relationship history 'stuff'; they thought that was pretty fast.

Were we sure?

Weren't we getting carried away?

It felt good, and we were determined to enjoy every minute, however long it would last.

Four days later, we had our first date; I saw him standing outside the bar we'd arranged to meet at – and I knew. It was like coming home. Our date lasted into the early hours of the following day – we talked and talked (okay, maybe we had a few kisses), and it felt like pure magic.

As we went our separate ways, it was like we had embarked upon a beautiful adventure. We were inseparable from this point on. Life got good, really fast.

Don't get me wrong; plenty of questions were hanging over our heads. Was this real? Did we honestly GET to be happy after everything we had both been through? (I would find out the extent of his story over time, although we shared so much even on our first date!), married for over 20 years with four children, oddly enough, they called time on their relationship within days of mine coming to an end the previous October).

We even had family holidays to the same places in our childhood! There were so many similarities between our stories; it was like our energy matched at every single level — no wonder I felt like I was being tickled by electricity on that first day!

We're like peas in a pod; we have a similar sense of humour, we are both a little nonsensical (aka fun) at times, we're much more relaxed around people once they get to know us, and we do love to entertain (in many different forms!).

Since 2017, we have gone on many incredible adventures together, always focusing on the things that make us happy. We have started two new businesses, plus taken on lots of other roles doing things that light us up, including singing in a 'Tuneless Choir'. In November 2021, after a covid-related postponement and a lot of 'will we/won't we time, we tied the knot in a magical, musical, thoroughly entertaining ceremony which brought love, laughter and real-life happy ever after to our friends and family, and our future continue to be bright and brilliant, together forever.

Now you're probably thinking, 'well, this all sounds very cute and fluffy, but what's the moral of this story?'

The moral is that everyone gets to have their happy ending, whatever it looks like if they are prepared to do the work!

Think about it for a moment. If you spend your life feeling sorry for yourself, focusing on the past and not learning anything from it, always more interested in what other people have that you don't - where will that get you? I could sit here and tell you many more stories about life-changing events I've been through that had a similar message. We always have a choice about how we move through challenges, what we take forward from them, and how we use them in our big life plans. If I had chosen something else at any point on this journey, all of this could have ended completely differently – but I would have been prepared to take responsibility for that.

Do you own what happens to you - or are you prepared to, from hereon in?

What changes can you make now on your path of self-discovery?

Sometimes the smallest, simplest decisions lead to the most wonderful discoveries – for example, that morning, I chose to go somewhere new. It was as if I understood this was the only way to experience something other than the disaster that felt like my life – and I followed that inner knowing.

When you choose YOU, above all else, here's what's possible: You could discover that saying yes to others always is saying no to yourself! Or that by moving your wants and needs higher up the list, it isn't just you who feels the benefit.

You could find that things you enjoy doing no longer make you feel guilty but instead have you enjoy the knowledge that there is always the possibility of 'more' at any time!

You might even realise that by being more honest about what you want, you can express yourself much more quickly to others, and in turn, your life lights up like Oxford Street at Christmas and makes you feel alive again! Wouldn't that be the most wonderful side effect? Sometimes in life, you must be prepared to leap into faith. Take the time to get to know who you are first, and then you'll be able to trust your choices with no doubts or wavering.

Be happy, comfortable, and content with who you are, LOVE who you are, and show up as the truest version of yourself.

You could surprise yourself with what you discover – and I, for one, would love to hear all about it!

KAREN FERGUSON

LIFETHERAPYUKCOACHING.COM

Chapter 4

I Am a Confident Woman

By Karen Ferguson

I wasn't always. In truth, I didn't feel confident when I was younger. I was taller than most and desperately didn't want to stand out from the crowd. I was kind of quiet because I thought this would attract less attention.

I was worried about getting things wrong or saying the wrong thing because I would have been terrified of being laughed at. I became two different people to feel comfortable around my two very different (and divorced) parents. I wanted to fit in, so I towed the line. I was not a confident girl.

That may be why I ended up being married to a man who seemed confident, strong and could look after me. And that is what he did until he didn't. Until the lies started, the financial abuse, the stealing, the accusations, the control.

—

I started to fade away. I forgot what happiness was. I got lost.

Then it got worse. I was diagnosed with Anaplastic Large Cell Lymphoma in April 2016, and my life came to a crashing halt. Not only did I need six rounds of chemo, but I was also so ill for the first two or three rounds that I spent more time in the hospital than I did out of it. It was often without any form of the immune system. Blood clots had been discovered in my lungs, so I had to inject myself with blood thinners every day, sometimes twice a day, when I needed to boost my immune system.

I was so sick that I was on two different types of anti-sickness tablets at the same time, but I still ended up dehydrated so often that I frequently required a drip to give me fluids because I couldn't drink enough.

I was so ill at one point from an infection that it was believed I had caught whilst in the hospital that I had two different antibiotics being pumped in from two different drips. My temperature was so high that I was hallucinating, and my now ex-husband got angry, told me I was selfish and left when I told him I didn't want to do this anymore. I didn't want to die; I just was tired from fighting the illness and the side effects of it all.

I had Sepsis, and he only said when I messaged him to tell him, 'You can die from that.' That was it, nothing else. No support, love, or understanding, just a bald and terrifying fact.

If I'm honest, I was kind of surprised to make it through the night, and I think a small part of me was disappointed that I had.

Despite the Sister's best efforts to keep me where I was, in a side room and, from my perspective at least, safe from catching anything else, I was moved.

I was told I would be in a side room, but then they tried to put me in a ward. I was terrified.

So there I was, a 40+ something woman, pretty much squashed into the corner of my bed, which was in the corridor of the ward, being looked at by staff and patients alike, absolutely distraught at the idea of being in with others and catching something else. I made a scene.

—

Previously I had been entirely comfortable with the idea that if I didn't need immediate help or attention and that someone else did, I was happy to wait. But not this time. I had been so ill that I could have died, and from something one of the numerous doctors had told me I had probably gotten from being on a ward, I could not afford to sit back and go along with what they told me. They seemed to have no real understanding of my fear.

It seemed that luck did smile on me a little that day, as the most senior nurse in the hospital happened to arrive, and when I explained the situation, she found me a bed in the private ward just a few hundred feet away.

My room, and finally, I began to feel safe.

I was there for a few days until I was told that the doctors didn't want to come and see me, so I had to return to the main ward. Again, the senior nurse did her best to keep me there. She saw no reason the doctors couldn't walk the few seconds required from the main to the private ward, but she was overruled, and I was moved.

Again, luck followed me, and I was put in a side room.

I recovered from Sepsis, and my treatment was reduced a little because my body was having a terrible time trying to cope with the drugs. I was also given antibiotics around the time of each treatment to prevent further infections.

It was a very strange time going through this process. It was as if I was the centre of attention but, at the same time, not important, at least not as a human being. I was often reduced to a name or medical condition; even then, people often got both wrong.

My notes were lost repeatedly, and if I hadn't known my treatment regime and the other drugs I was on, I honestly dread what might have happened.

I remember one lovely doctor looking after me when I was once again in A&E, asking me about my drugs and when I listed everything, he smiled and said, 'You know more than I do about this.'

He was right, but I had learnt that I had to.

Maybe having to stand up for me, despite being ill and whilst being bald from the drugs, triggered something in me. Perhaps this is why I found my confidence, fight, and desire to not just put up with things anymore.

I fought for others as well. I made a huge complaint to the hospital; I didn't think it was right that others might have to go through what I did. The interview was recorded, and I was asked if it could be played to the relevant staff as it was thought hearing my experiences would make more impact than just reading a report. I said they could play it to anyone they considered necessary if they thought it would help.

I was told they planned to make specific training and process changes because of my complaint. I don't know if they did, but I had to speak out because not everyone was like me, and not everyone would have the capacity I did to stand up for myself.

As a result of my illness and treatment, my GP, when I finally saw her again, told me that because of me and the difficulties around getting a diagnosis, it took six or seven months and finally a biopsy to decide what was wrong, that she had now changed the way she dealt with unusual symptoms. I think I made a difference!

Not only that, but again, thanks to my GP, I was invited to attend the surgery as an expert patient, to speak to student doctors about my experience because she (my GP) said that she believed hearing my story from me would have a much longer lasting effect on them, than simply hearing a case study.

I hope I made a difference. Life was never the same again, and I don't just mean my health.

During my treatment, I found out that my husband, who had taken six months of work to look after me, had borrowed quite a lot of money from two family members, telling them it was to help me and pay the bills.

Only he didn't use it to pay the bills, or at least not the mortgage. My share of the bills was still being paid, and I was still doing my best to work when I could, but he not only didn't work, he spent a fair chunk of the money he had borrowed on buying a motorbike. He later had to sell a bike at a loss to pay back the person he had bought it from, a local man who kept turning up on the doorstep asking for his money.

My confidence was starting to rear its head now. This time I wouldn't be helping to bail him out. This time I was taking away all major bills and paying them from my account.

This was when I started to hide my money from him. I stopped telling him what I had learnt or how much I had. I stopped taking up the slack from his inability or perhaps unwillingness to manage money like an adult.

He didn't like it one bit.
He pushed and pushed and pushed, and then…

One day, and I honestly cannot tell you what happened or why, I decided that I had had enough of this, that I wanted to be happy, to be me, whoever that was, and I started to change.

I'm not going to tell you that it was this explosive moment where I grabbed hold of life and let it carry me away, as amazing as that would have been. But some of the smaller things made me first notice a difference. I started to wear lipstick again, got my nails done, and began to write, and it was as much a surprise to me as anyone else that I could write; not only that, but it seemed that I was funny too.

And who would have thought that after the release of my first book, I would be working towards a career as a writer? I never thought I was any good at writing, even though I've written and co-written so many courses that I've forgotten. I never had the confidence to believe in myself. I took comments far too personally.

I felt every negative comment was a devastating blow to my self-esteem. I felt criticised and knocked down. I honestly thought that I wasn't good enough.

But my growing confidence had changed this. Don't get me wrong; I still had moments of doubt. I still question myself and set high standards for myself, but this is an ever-changing journey, and I have more amazing days than negative ones.

I had changed, and fading into the background was no longer enough; I wanted more. I wanted my voice, to be comfortable being the centre of attention; I wanted a life.

I held myself accountable for improving my life. I stopped backing down for an 'easy' life. I stopped agreeing simply because it was easier, and I started to get louder.

I did my best to push him out of my life, and he went for a while, but then he returned.

I didn't want him back, but the pressure was relentless, and I gave in, only to quickly realise I had made a major mistake.

I learnt, though. I learnt how to deal with him. He kept pushing me back into being relatively quiet and lacking in confidence the woman he thought I was, or at least who he thought he was more able to control.

But he failed. I wouldn't let him.

I stood my ground; I got him out, pressed charges, kept my determination and confidence, and even when he drove his car into my house, I fought to stay the new, more confident version of myself.

I faced him in court, and god did I shake, but I stood my ground. I faced the sleepless nights, nightmares and PTSD symptoms medication free because I knew I had to go through this to come out the other side, and I knew that despite the days of shaking and the waves of panic that hit suddenly, I would get through this.

I won.

I spoke up; I said no; I said yes; I shared my story, my experiences, my pain even, but I spoke up, and I started to make a difference.

I started to sing, not in public, and probably not very tunefully, but I loved it. I even began to sing in my kitchen, in front of my children, something I had never done because my home has never been a place where I felt secure enough to be happy, where joy was frowned upon.

———

I learned new skills, gained more qualifications, broadened my social network, made new friends, became an ambassador for a domestic abuse charity, went on some dates, and found my feet, focus, and passion. I pushed myself into new situations and environments, I did things that made me nervous, and I allowed myself to be vulnerable and test out the waters of trusting someone again. I pushed myself to start being all those things I had always wanted to be.

Now I relish being on stage, talking to, encouraging, motivating and helping hundreds, if not thousands, of people at a time.

I know what it is like to feel all those negative emotions, and I know what it is like to be filled with confidence, to have great self-esteem, to know my value, my worth and the important role I play in this life. I know how to make a difference.

How life has changed because now, I love being centre stage, I love who I am, what I do, and how my life is going. I love that I found myself and my voice, and I am

—

so delighted that I can now say and mean that I am a confident woman.

Karen Ferguson

Author, Coach, Ambassador & Motivator

www.lifetherapyukcoaching.com

lifetherapyukcoaching@gmail.com

https://www.facebook.com/iamkarenferguson

07718 144078

LAURA BILLINGHAM

WORD-WITCH.CO.UK

Chapter 5

Finding My Story

By Laura Billingham

Some time ago, I was asked to contribute to a book about making 360 degree career changes, and it prompted me to look back at my life.

As a small child, I was bright, chatty, confident and insanely imaginative (imaginary friends, pretend games and constantly making up stories). Starting primary school in the term before my 5th birthday marked a turning point; I quickly realised that to fit in, it is easier to be the same as everyone else, to not stand out but disappear in the crowd and (at school anyway) I became the very epitome of the good little girl.

Although bright, I didn't start school being able to read, it was actually the second year of infant school before the black marks in books suddenly coalesced into meaning they were ways of telling stories!

WOW!

That was a pivotal moment for me, and I raced through every book in the school in record time. By age 7, I was writing poems and stories, and by the time the final year of primary school began, I was more or less left to my own devices during English lessons as I'd completed all the lesson workbooks and read all the books in the school!

My love of the written word led teachers (and fellow pupils) at my secondary school to label me as clever, swotty tags that stuck to me. I was pushed towards academia and told by teachers, career advisors and even my parents that it was too hard to make a living doing what I loved, i.e., writing stories. So, I left school at age 16 and went to an FE College to study Business (a minor act of rebellion in that I refused A Levels and university) and began working aged 18, first in the civil service, then as a travel agent in a university and later in office management.

I did the usual settle down and have children thing, and my storytelling became confined to bedtimes with my daughters. Work was simply a means to an end, and I trudged on, eventually doing quite well and reaching the dizzy heights of Operations Manager for a large software company.

I have no doubt that life would have continued in the same vein except for a couple of events in 2014, my mum (who had been acting oddly for a couple of years) was diagnosed with Alzheimers, and then, in 2015, I moved out to a tiny village in the Peak District. These two events forced me to take stock, and I realised I simply couldn't commute to a stressful job AND be available if mum needed me. I decided to opt for redundancy and try to work out a way to earn money from home.

During the 6 months I was able to take without looking to earn anything, I was able to complete a novel to first draft level and also to enter NaNoWriMo (write 50,000 words in a month). Finances called though (rather urgently actually) and I started a part-time role whilst organising a franchise to work as a virtual assistant. By October 2016 I was self-employed.

Unfortunately, I quickly realised that VA (virtual assistant) work under the constraints of a franchise was not for me. Having to act like a clone of all the other VAs in the network in order to meet the franchise agreement didn't sit well with me! I tried, really tried, for over a year until, in April 2018, I attended a day-long event organised by someone I know. It was a business boot-camp, with lots of hints and tips etc. However, the only new thing I learnt that day was that I truly had no passion for my business; the other attendees so obviously loved what they did, yet I felt flat and uninspired.

A period of self-reflection followed, during which time I stumbled across EAM (Energy Alignment Method) and began to use it to work through my self-belief (or rather lack of) as regards to using my writing to earn a living. I also realised, after attending a two-day course on EAM, that I am destined for bigger things although I'm still not exactly sure what!

The result of all this navel gazing and energy work was that in July 2018, I literally pushed the f**k it button jacked in the franchise and began to offer writing services. I hit lucky when a referral led to a small contract, and other work followed.

Because I LOVE what I do now, I am able to get out there and sell myself and my services with a real passion - and it shows. I'm sure this positive energy attracts clients to me.

In tandem with my writing, my partner has trained to be a voice-over artist and has all the kit to produce professionally recorded material for corporate videos, games, telephone systems, and the like. His business sits under mine, and I manage his bookings.

My dream of writing novels has also been resurrected; my first, a timeslip, was published in January 2019 and has five-star reviews on Amazon. Even in the lockdowns of 2020, I was able to write, completing a challenge of thirty-one stories during the month of May. These were published as an anthology later that year. With another slight change of direction, I am now also heavily involved in helping other fledging authors see their dreams of writing and publishing become a reality.

To all of you reading this, I would caution you to NEVER give up on your dreams; it's never too late to start over. I only wish the education sector would stop focusing on academia, we aren't all destined to be high-achieving graduates. We should equip our children with the necessary tools to allow them to find their own path. It may well be convoluted and twisty, but it should be theirs to find, not officialdom to dictate. And who knows, one day, the arts and writing may be considered as valid a career path as other more academic professions.

Laura Billingham
Word Witch
www.word-witch.co.uk
07736 351341

LAVINIA MILNER-GRAY

ORIGINOFENERGYCOACHING.COM

Chapter 6

Life and Expectations

By Lavinia Milner-Gray

Life is mostly peaceful with more frequent moments of joy and fulfilment. That is my life now, however it wasn't always like that.

Life is full of tragedy, challenges, happiness and joy. My life has been a roller coaster ride of experiences and emotions for the most part. That's what makes life, life, I guess.

We grow up with the expectation that life is an easy road with a couple of turns and little bumps along the way. The reality is that life isn't always that way and I have come to believe it's our expectations that let us down. Expectations to have a wonderful childhood full of fun, warm, and loving memories. Expectations that as we grow up, we will always have our family and friends throughout our lives without experiencing any loss or pain. Expectations that things will always stay the same and the happy experiences will last forever.

Well life isn't like that and my experiences certainly had lots of ups, downs, pain, love and loss. I have learnt that part of my pain and struggle through life has been because my expectations have not been met.

I've carried many painful memories of losing immediate family members as young as 11 years old. I lost my father unexpectedly. That was an absolute blow.

Again, at the age of 16 I lost my 10-year-old nephew (who I considered my brother we were so close), tragically in a crocodile attack and at the age of 23 (I think) I lost my sister who took her life. I don't readily recall what age I lost my sister as the pain of losing loved ones suddenly and tragically was unbearable and my way of coping was to block the memories and forget. Not long after my brothers passing, I moved with my family from Zambia to Australia. That was a tough time, learning to live with my family again, as I had been at boarding school since the age of 12. There were so many changes that I felt were happening all at once.

My early life was spent in Zambia. My parents were farmers and I grew up on a farm with my parents and siblings. I had a wonderful childhood, spent outdoors with friends, exploring the neighbouring farms and getting up to all sorts of mischief, innocent mischief I might add.

Our imaginations used to run wild playing house with a few tins and mud. Building a BMX track in the bush and riding around the farm. It was so much fun. It was the days when the 5pm bell used to ring was when we knew it was time to go home and I would run across the fields, jump over fences and at times if not careful checking which field I was crossing at the time would get chased by a bull. Those were the days when you fell down, got up, dusted yourself off and kept going. The carefree days when there was nothing to worry about but just being a child.

My life changed when one of my older sisters received a phone call one dreads. My father had passed away suddenly. I was 11 years old and I felt like my world had suddenly turned into something I no longer understood. It was the first time I had experienced grief. It was such a strange feeling which was totally unexpected and I didn't know how to react. It felt like I had left my body and someone else was having those experiences. I was on holiday in one of the bigger towns in Zambia with my sister.

It was just a normal afternoon when we received the call. My sister and I jumped into her car to go back home to the farm.

What was normally an hour and a half drive felt like five hours.

It was the longest drive home trying to figure out what to expect when I got there, seeing my Mum and my other siblings.

It was the longest drive of my life and the days that incurred are one long emotional blur. It was probably that experience that taught me how to bury unpleasant memories that over the years were soon a blank.

A few years after having lost my Dad, at the age of 16 my family and I experienced another terrible blow. I lost my 10-year-old nephew (as far as I was concerned, he was my brother as he had lived with us on the farm and we were as thick as thieves), tragically in a crocodile attack. I lived with the guilt of not being with him when it happened. I always looked out for him and on that fatal weekend I didn't accompany him and family friends on a weekend away water skiing at a lake. I felt numb when we received the call. I couldn't quite comprehend what was happening. It happened to be the same time my family and I had decided to migrate to Australia.

Him and I were so excited about our new life and all the fun we were going to have living close to the beach. I felt like my heart had been ripped from my chest.

This was a different sort of grief to losing my father. I suppose it could have been he was so young and had so much ahead of him. I had not expected to experience so much grief at my young age.

The only way I knew how to deal with the loss was to bury the grief and blank the memory of the time leading up to and after his death.

Only now years later have I had the courage to seek help and allow those memories to be seen and experienced in order to forgive and move forward.

Not long after my brothers passing, I moved with my family from Zambia to Australia. That was a tough time, learning to live with my family again. I had been away at boarding school since the age of 12 only coming home for the holidays every three or four months. I was going through so many changes.

I left behind all that was familiar, my home, my friends and my extended family whom I was close to. The move came with its fair share of challenges. I had to decide what I was going to do with my life, go to college, university or work? I had to make new friends and find my way around a new town. The lifestyle was quite different to what I was used to.

I had moved from living on a farm and going to a boarding school in a rural farming area to a fairly big down on the coast.

Australia at that time was a little different to how it is now. It had only been about 10 years since the "White Australia" policy had been lifted so it was a novelty for many to see a mixed-race young African woman in the town.

I experienced a fair share of racism. A memory that always stick in my mind was being called a "Jungle Bunny". I can laugh at that memory now however if I'm being honest it took me many many years to forgive that person for making me feel I wasn't worthy and good enough. From that day on I always felt like I stood out and I think from that experience I learnt to become invisible. Prior to that I had been confident and it didn't worry me what people thought. Learning to be invisible also led to behaviours of becoming a people pleaser because I wanted to be liked and not feel different to the people around me.

Whilst living in Australia I lost my sister who took her life, I think I was 23 years old then. I don't immediately recall what age I lost my sister as the pain of losing loved ones suddenly and tragically was too much for me to bear and new my way of coping which was working was to shut down and forget.

After all my experiences I started to hate the sound of the phone ringing expecting it to bring more bad news.

My 20's soon became all about "partying". I dabbled in recreational drugs and alcohol. I know the constant "partying" helped block out the grief. It was my way of coping and keeping the memories buried deep.

I had suicidal thoughts however I didn't follow through with trying anything as deep down I knew that life is beautiful even with its pain.

I went through a series of ups and downs over the years, not feeling like I belonged anywhere. Moving from one city to the next on the east coast of Australia was exciting, although it didn't quite address what I was going through. There were a lot of fun times, making new friends and discovering new places. Those periods of happiness did not last long and I was going through a particularly challenging stage mentally when my family thought it best for me to go to England for a couple of years. It was a good opportunity for me to break the cycle I was in. For some reason I felt more like I belonged in England and years later after a past life experience I understood why.

During my journey of healing, I had the wonderful opportunity to meet an emotional healer and experience a past life.

The life I saw was a version of me on a swing in a beautiful quintessential English garden in the summer. On that swing I was filled with deep inner peace. A peace I had not experienced for many many years. It may be no surprise that after going back to Australia for a few years I returned to live in England six years ago and now live in a quintessential English village.

After I returned to Australia from England, I met a man who became my husband ten months after our first meeting. I know it sounds corny but "when it's meant to be its meant to be". I certainly wasn't looking for love then. My plan was to complete my university degree I had started prior to my departure to England and begin my corporate career. My life had taken an unexpected turn and I was ready for it.

What came next was a series of challenges this time in my corporate career. I worked in corporate banking in a male dominated environment and I believed the only way to fit in and be accepted was to become one of the "boys". It meant working late nights, excessive drinking accompanied with an unhealthy diet trying to counteract the heavy nights.

Living that lifestyle started to take its toll on my health both physically and mentally. Trying to be one of the "boys' didn't help my career progression.

I later found out that my career was intentionally hindered because I ticked the boxes of what made up a diverse team. I was a woman of colour and being the only woman and only person that was non-white I ticked two boxes making the team "diverse". This came as yet another blow. I was being deliberately held back from fulfilling my potential because of the colour of my skin. Again, race played a part in my life as it did years before and fuelled the feeling of not being worthy and not being enough.

It was about that time when I felt I was stagnating that I started to experience panic attacks. It started off with one or two however over time they became more frequent. Upon reflection on my life's experience, I realised I was carrying so much trauma. The panic attacks were a message for me to start taking care of myself and heal the pain I had been carrying for so long. I had been through so much tragedy and loss from a young age and I had buried it deep so as not to face the pain. I had felt less than and had disconnected from my confidence because it was pointed out to me that I was different to everyone else and this was done in a negative, belittling way.

Finally, I reached a pivotal moment in my life. I remember that day clearly. I was at my desk at work when suddenly my vision blurred, my chest tightened making it difficult to breath.

My heart was racing and I felt dizzy and was sweating profusely.

At first, I had no idea what was happening to me because I had never experienced anything like it. I always felt somewhat in control even when I had experienced previous panic attacks. This one was different; one I had never experienced before. I managed to gather myself after what seemed like hours and somehow got myself to the bathroom and as I lay on the floor in the cubicle trying to ground myself, I decided then that something if not everything in my life had to change. This experience scared me to the core as I grew up with people close to me who had suffered from depression and alcoholism. I was terrified of going down that road myself.

I summed up the courage and asked for help. Up until that point I thought I could manage these experiences and keep burying the trauma deep down in my body. I realised I couldn't do it on my own and my journey to healing began. I was ready for change and to accept the experiences that life had given me. I was ready to let go of the trauma and forgive all the experiences that hadn't met my expectations. My journey of counselling, therapy, coaching, spiritual and emotional healing began. This journey began several years ago and each modality has helped me in different ways.

I am learning to accept the life I have been given and that I always have a choice. A choice in how I choose to live my life. Upon reflection of my experiences, they have made me compassionate, empathic, resilient and adaptable. This path of self-healing and self-discovery has helped me realise and accept that this is part of the journey. The experiences as traumatic as they have been have shaped who I am today. I have learnt that death is part of life. I no longer fear it and have come to accept it. If anything, it has helped me become more grateful for this beautiful gift of life.

My life is changing, every day I am developing a deeper understanding of Self. My self-love is getting deeper and that in turn has benefitted my relationships. The different methods of therapy and healing have showed me the only way out of the pain is through the pain. The root to resolving pain is not to run away from it but to move towards it as difficult as it can be at times. I've learnt to lean into my experience of life, my journey.

Every opportunity that presents itself I see as a gift, a chance to learn, been seen and heard and to be my true authentic self. An opportunity to push my boundaries and in doing so my life is more fulfilling and filled with more frequent moments of joy. Each day I take the time to reflect on my life thus far and right now I am living my best life.

—

I have solid, loving relationships with my husband, children, family and friends. My career which has transformed over the years and is going in the direction I was aspiring it to. Being ready to let go, forgive and live in gratitude has opened unexpected doors for me. Doors that have led to some amazing experiences.

Is my healing complete, honestly not yet.
There is still work to be done however I definitely love, honour and respect myself for everything I have experienced in this life and I do experience more joy and inner peace. I honour myself for having the courage to seek help, support and guidance to live an incredible life. Life is made up of fun, loss, love and joy and when we accept this it opens the door to living an incredible life.

MILA JOHANSEN

MILAJOHANSEN.COM

Chapter 7

Daydreams Really Do Come True

By Mila Johansen

From poverty to abundance, from hungry child to organic farmer, from daydreams to success. The small child who didn't pay attention in school, against all odds, became a successful writer, teacher, and public speaker.

Everything that happened to me built my character. Many of the events that took place in my life as a child became the cornerstones of who I have become today. The "Cinderella" in our household growing up, I did all the housework in our home, about four hours a day, from the age of ten.

I often went to school without lunch and watched as all the kids who sat before me feasted on sack lunches. I grew up in a very meagre, poor home with a single mother who was a third-grade teacher, which is part of why I'm a teacher today. She would leave at six in the morning and drive forty minutes to set up her classroom for her teaching job. So, at a very young age, I had to get my brother up, make sure he got breakfast, and move us both out the door to walk a mile to school. Bobby was two and a half years younger than me. When we were very young, we often went to bed without dinner. Now I appreciate every single thing that is given to me.

I was a "glass half-full" kind of girl from the beginning. The very first movie I saw in a theatre was *Pollyanna* at the age of seven. That one movie affected me in so many ways. For one thing, I came home wishing there was a big screen on my bedroom wall to watch Pollyanna whenever I wanted. I hadn't seen any other movie, except every Sunday night, we went across the street to my grandmother's house to watch Disney's *Sunday Night Movies*. Now, it's amazing that we can watch anything we want anytime. I often still marvel at that.

So, my life has been a lot like the "Pollyanna" attitude in the movie—the "Glad Game." At one point, she tells the story of a time with her father. Pollyanna wanted a doll, so her father said, "Let's go look in the church donation barrel." The only item they found that day was a pair of crutches. So, he said, "Let's play the Glad Game. Let's think of something to be glad for about finding the crutches." Pollyanna thought for a minute and said, "Well, I guess I can be glad I don't need the crutches."

And that has always been my attitude with so many things. I'm not afraid to admit that I am a real live Pollyanna. For some reason, I've always thought I could have everything. My life was great, and nothing seemed to get me down. Maybe I often went hungry, but I always remained positive.

I want to tell you about a fantastic experience I had. . . I must have been a "glass half-full" girl even back then. I didn't realise I practised manifesting even in those days.

We drove to church every Sunday, and on the way, next to the freeway, there was an A-frame house. It was like a cabin, but big, with two stories. I loved it, and I thought, *I want that house.* I was eight. I wanted to live in that house. So, I started daydreaming about how I could get it. I tried to make the money I needed to buy it. Even at eight years old, I thought I could have that house. Of course, I didn't get the house . . .then.

I asked my mother to stop one Sunday, and we went on a tour inside. A big sign we could read from the freeway read "Open House". So, we went in and looked around. I continued daydreaming that I could somehow have that house someday.

Around the same time, at age eight or nine, I wanted to be a writer. I wanted to be a writer more than I wanted to be anything else. We went to see *Mary Poppins*, another one of the first movies I ever went to; there weren't a lot of movies back then. We finally had a TV, one of those old-fashioned brown box, furniture-looking things, with about three channels.

When I came home from the movie, I went into my bedroom, shut the door, and secretly made some chalk drawings—as I had seen in the film. I closed my eyes and tried to jump in.

I believed I could jump into the chalk drawings and be transported to a beautiful, magical world full of greenery, flowers, merry-go-rounds, and penguins. It didn't work. I tried at least five times. They were probably pitiful drawings because I've never been an artist and managed more than poorly drawn stick figures.

I wanted to be a writer and create magic that way. I loved to read *Nancy Drew* and *The Bobbsey Twins*. My mother read me all fourteen of the OZ books by Frank Baum. She had the entire set of hardbound volumes from her childhood in England. Later I read them all to myself.

The same day I made the chalk drawings, I started writing a book. I wrote a page and a half and quit— because I was eight. But I knew then that I wanted to be a writer. Later on in life, when I became a playwright, I wrote the first three OZ books into stunning musicals that have been performed on many community theatre stages.

At age 18, my mother tricked me into becoming a writer. She said, "Mila, I know you have always wanted to be a writer, so why don't you write just one sentence daily for a month." I agreed, thinking I could stick to writing one sentence daily. But it turned out I needed more than one sentence. It's like potato chips, I found myself writing a page or two or more, and by the end of the month—I was a writer. Voila!

I always daydreamed. I don't think teachers liked me because my head lived in the clouds. I could never pay attention. I remember looking out the windows at the clouds marching by, imagining myself dancing on top of them. Now I realize I spent my school days daydreaming about my future life. I spent those years sharpening my imagination and learning exactly what I needed for my future life as a writer.

I even started daydreaming about the man I was destined to meet. I started speaking to the stars—to the man I knew I would eventually marry. I lay in the curve of a large dolphin statue in a nearby park, looked up into the Milky Way Galaxy, and spoke out loud. I knew he waited out there for me. I knew him as if I had already met him.

I kept speaking to him, and when I went to a four-year college, I met him in the most extraordinary way. We joined the same intramural coed baseball team that a mutual friend had put together. I showed up for the very first game of the season, and no one came but one person, Rich. We had never met before that day and started talking. Within five minutes, I knew I wanted to be part of his life.

We finally had to officially forfeit the game since only two of us showed up. We shrugged and began walking in different directions: me towards home, and he headed towards the campus buildings. I suddenly turned around, caught up to him, and said, "Where are you going?" He said he wanted to work on his painting in the art department. I went along to see his work.

I told him I had a weekly dancing date that night with my girlfriend and asked if he wanted to meet me there. He did, and we started dating. He courted me by dropping off boxes of oranges on my doorstep.

Later, I married him. He's an organic farmer, so I never went hungry again. We've been married for forty-three years now—one of the main abundances of my life. By the way, the rest of the team showed up to every other game after that fateful day.

When I met my husband, Rich, he put me to work on his family's organic citrus ranch. Lucky for him, he got a "Cinderella" because I had done that four hours a day of work at my house growing up. My brother only did a half hour a week—taking out the trash and mowing the tiny tract home lawn, which ruined him. He didn't make it out of our neighbourhood. He ended up being a casualty of our childhood in "gangland." I'm certain I survived because I became a worker and partly due to my extreme naivety.

So, when I got to the citrus ranch, I didn't mind doing all the work. When I saw all the fruit, the number twos (substandard for selling), I said, "Rich, there's so much extra fruit, we've got to give it away."

He said, "No, no, no, Mila. We don't give anything away."

Rich is the most generous person I know, but his family came out of the depression era and lived in that consciousness, even though they earned very good money, owning several businesses.

I insisted, "Oh yeah, we're going to give it away." In the long run, I won out, and now we give 10,000 to 20,000 pounds a year to local food banks.

My grandmother was my Fairy Godmother. I spent much of my childhood listening to entertaining stories of her childhood and later adventures. Jessie Haver Butler, a very famous suffragette, who became the first woman lobbyist at the Capitol in Washington DC, came from a tragic childhood on a Colorado cattle ranch. (When I compare my childhood with hers, I count mine as a blessing.)

A teacher saw Jessie's brightness and helped her get into Smith College in New England, where she thrived. In her first job after graduating from Smith, she helped Professor Cunliffe put together the Pulitzer School of Journalism at Columbia.

In her second job, she helped set the first minimum wage in the country for women, from $4.00 a week to $8.00; at the same time, she worked hard to get children out of the factories.

In Washington DC, she became the first official woman lobbyist and worked closely with Alice Paul and Carrie Chapman Catt to help women win the right to vote in 1920. She later spoke all over London with George Bernard Shaw and taught Eleanor Roosevelt to speak.

She was destined to be on the front lines and part of many historical events. In her early nineties, she shared the podium several times with Gloria Steinem and Marlo Thomas and took me along. She half-raised me, which is why I turned out the way I have. Jessie and I were always together, joined at heart.

To inspire us all, she gave her last speech in Hollywood at age 94, then let her secretary go and passed away at 98. Through regular walking, swimming, and vitamins, Jessie mastered the art of reinventing herself until the very end.

Because of knowing her, I've always said, even at eighteen, "I'm going to make a great old lady because I'm already eccentric." Jessie is the perfect example that it doesn't matter where we come from or what has happened to us; we can raise ourselves and become anything.

Even though I grew up in poverty, I always had a generous heart. If one of my friends liked my blouse, I'd give it to her; I could get another one at the thrift store. I always feel that the more I give—which is one of my secrets—the more I get. But that's not why I do it. Giving seems like a puzzle, especially when no one knows about it. I treat it like a game to see how much I can give without getting caught. Besides, the more you give, the more you receive. There's enough for everyone—we must tap into the funnel to send it our way.

In my younger years, my consciousness scored low on the money scale. I didn't think I could have much money at that point; I felt I didn't deserve it. I've met many other people who have felt the same way. I've worked hard for every penny I've earned.

We scrimped and saved for years. I remember never having more than a dollar in my pocket. Then Rich and I started going to La Jolla, in Southern California, to visit with part of his family who lived in the hills above the opulent town. They weren't particularly wealthy. After about three years of walking through the streets of La Jolla every summer, I started realizing, "Wow, I could have some of this; this is for everybody." I started feeling that I belonged there. Even though I often came straight from boogie boarding in the ocean and went to La Jolla dressed in my ragged shorts, flip-flops, and a tunic.

I'd walk through the stores where owners weren't pleased to see me because I probably didn't buy anything. It raised my consciousness that I would have money someday; I started getting that into my head and thinking about it and asking for it in my meagre way, though I've learned better ways now to do it.

I kept daydreaming—that's the most important thing. I had to visualize new things.

I daydreamed about becoming a published writer. Another technique I started using was writing down lists of things I wished for and wanted to happen. Someone along the way shared that technique with me, so I did it. I made my first list, which had things like directing plays, writing books, and making more money. It also had some basics, like flossing more and eating healthier. I wanted to be a published author. I wanted to teach classes. I had some impossible things in there, too. Two years later, in my late twenties, I looked at that list, and everything had come true.

So now I'm making new lists. And every time I make a list, when I go back to it—maybe even ten years later—all of it has come to fruition. Sometimes, the things you dream of and wish for don't come true immediately. They come true when you need them. I didn't realize I was manifesting all through my life—starting with not paying attention in grade school.

One important thing I did learn was in high school during my senior year. I mastered finger placement and typing. A very good thing for a writer.

It's practically the only thing I learned because it was kinesthetic, and it turns out I'm a kinesthetic learner.

Everyone should have to learn finger placement. I can't believe how many people I know don't have that skill.

Then I started manifesting in a big way! I became a landscaper/gardener for a few years in addition to working on the citrus ranch. At the same time, I taught dance, a lot of dance. And I started teaching kids. I began teaching an after-school theatre program. I became a kind of "Jill" of all trades. These days, everyone is spouting, "Multiple streams of income." That's precisely what I did way back then. Now I talk about how to create and juggle "multiple streams of income."

During landscaping jobs, I began daydreaming about how much money I wanted to make. I remember the exact amount—$500 a day. That became my goal. I couldn't believe it, but in two or three years, I brought in $500 a day through my ranch work and sales, combined with other endeavours.

That turned out to be a huge amount back then. So, it came true. But I had first said, "I'm going to do it," and believed in it. I've experienced many manifestations, but that was one of my first significant, concentrated manifestations.

Remember that A-frame house? Recently, in the last eight years, my father-in-law needed to move in with us. We had always lived with him on the citrus ranch during harvests, and we knew we loved him and lived well together. At ninety years of age, he offered to help us build a house on our smaller farm in the foothills so he could move in. We built a big home near Nevada City in the foothills above Sacramento, California.

One day I went down to pick lavender below our new home. I looked back at the house, which I had never done before. I couldn't believe it! The house was the A-frame house from my childhood, but three times as big— precisely the same house. I realized I had manifested it, but it took decades to happen. I thought that turned out to be funny and profound and a major abundance in my life.

Daydreams hold a fantastic amount of power. One day, I looked back and realized that every dream I had imagined had come true. I needed to start remembering to dream new daydreams, to keep manifesting and creating the future.

RAMONA STRONACH

TAP YOUR POSSIBLE

Chapter 8

You are the Path

By Ramona Stronach

Day 3; April 2nd, 2004 Walk from Arrens-Marsous to Gourette, Pyrenees, France.

Journal excerpt: one of our most mental, physical and challenging times.

The panic surged like a bolt of electricity when we realised what we were up against. We could just about see the greyish stones dotted along the edge of the extremely high mountain pass road in the Pyrenees that separated the sheer vertical drop beyond them and the narrow road that hugged the side of the mountain.

The tone in my brother's voice set every muscle in my body on edge when he was the first to connect those stones and the predicament we were in.

The four of us had emerged from a steep climb that begun not far from the accommodation that housed us the night before in the village of Arrens.

After breakfast, we set out under the grey pallor of the morning sky to undertake the approximately 2-hour walk to our destination of Gourette along the mountain road that the friendly owner of our accommodation, who couldn't do enough for us when he recognised us as pilgrims by the scallop shells attached to our rucksacks, had indicated it would take.

As we ascended the steep climb and left the village behind, the rain came upon us, and we dodged puddles of water that soon turned into streams beneath our feet. The air was becoming colder. Suddenly, the snow emptied itself onto us and hit our faces. The cold was sharp against my face.

By the time we reached the end of the climb, the snow had descended and we were deposited onto an opening up of the land where we could see the road through the white fuzz. The silence was deep in the expansive scenery ahead of us. Nothing moved except the snow.

In the distance, the road snaked its way along the mountainside to a point where the bend in the road blocked the view. This was the road we were due to walk along. Yet something was not quite right with it.

When our eyes had adjusted to and taken in the expanse of snowy white peaks against the horizon, we could see that the road was blocked by snow, and its drift had stopped just short of the stones. Moments later, it had sunk in. We were in a compromised position. We looked back to see if we could return the way we had come. But the snow had disorientated the landscape behind us and the wind was whipping it into a blizzard.

Surely the locals that we met the day before must have known the pass was closed when their interest in us was piqued when they found out we were walking to Santiago De Compostela and were planning to walk to Gourette the following day. The conversations had been somewhat disjointed in French and English; perhaps something must have become lost in translation because we definitely shouldn't have been up there. Time seemed to white out like the scenery all around us.

It felt like we were debating how to get out of this situation for a long time but it was probably only a few minutes. Surely, we could ring the emergency services? What was the national SOS number for France?

None of us knew. Two of us had mobiles. No signal.

I don't remember how we decided to walk along the road's edge. I remember the fear. I wanted to be anywhere but there, back in the safety of Arrens.

This was supposed to be a road walk, not a snow walk. This wasn't what I signed up for when I hijacked, along with my sister, my father's plan to walk an ancient pilgrim trail across North Spain with my brother hopping on last minute. There was no way we would let father do that alone. What if he got lost? But this 'what if' had not been on the cards.

I was terrified of heights. I wanted to run. Run far away from the fear of what my mind was alerting me to. The fear of one of us slipping; what if there was ice on top of those stones? What if we could only get so far along them? The fear of the wind suddenly getting stronger and knocking us off balance leapt through my mind. The fear of a sudden blizzard while on the edge of that road shrieked at me. The fear of someone else panicking whilst we were making our way over those stones. No one knew where we were. The fear of not being in control fully landed in my body.

These thoughts flooded my mind in seconds, but I was allowing them to keep me in fear.

All time seemed to stop as we each took our first step onto the first stone. Amazingly the snow did too. There is nothing like a survival situation forcing you into the present moment where the placing of the feet and constant assessment of the next move are consciously made. The soles of my feet felt like they were glued to the inner soles of my walking boots, willing them to cling to the surface of those stones.

The Present Moment - where we can consciously create from this space if we are to avoid making a life with projections from our past or concerns about our future. There was no space for thoughts about the future here, though. Do not let go of focus was the mantra my mind repeated.

My eyes didn't dare move to the right of me. I knew the sheer drop was right there.

Instead, I kept my eyes on the contour of the snow on the road to the left of me. Sometimes the snow was at knee level; at other times, the drift was at shoulder height. There were some parts of the road where the snow lay shallow or didn't quite reach it, which gave us some respite from that edge.

The air was perfectly still. It was like the atmosphere was holding its breath as it witnessed our challenge. We hardly spoke except for my father's or my sister's words of encouragement because of the need for sheer concentration. So much so that I forgot the heaviness of my rucksack and the back aches from the previous day's trek from Lourdes to Arrens that had been stunning but physically challenging for me as I had ridiculously overpacked my rucksack; as someone who had never had to rely on living out of the contents of one before, I thought I had packed sensibly. My body didn't.

When that road left behind the sheer drop for a while as it wound into a bend, which was our exit off it, father fell.

We all shrieked. If my father had lost his footing earlier on... It was the release of energy that we all needed. My heart soon sank when I realised the next challenge was mocking us; we had a climb over the top of a mountain facing us. As if life didn't want to challenge us enough. We could not risk continuing on the road; we could not risk the prospect of being stuck on the edge of D918.

A signpost pointing to a national pathway that headed up the mountain provided some relief; we weren't so off the beaten track amongst the mountainous landscape all around us.

The mountain. It, too, is firmly etched in my memory field. Beautiful, hostile, astounding and intimidating. All these qualities rolled into one peak. The fear raced up from within again. What if there was another avalanche? I felt the wind whip up around us as my father pointed to the col of the mountain we had to reach, reassuring us that Gourette was on the other side.

You had to be kidding. On either side of the small neck of this mountain were enormous outcrops of jagged rocks. Now and then, in between patches of blue sky, grey clouds skidded over the col covering it up menacingly. What if we missed the col because of sudden bad weather and got lost? What if there was another mountain to overcome, and my father was wrong?

The fear felt different this time. I felt safer being away from the road. My concerns turned to the physical challenge of the mountain climb.

The path meandered up from the road. The snow hadn't quite fully covered it. My anxiety arose again the more we ascended; we didn't know how much of a climb was ahead of us. I was anxious about getting off that mountain before evening fall, especially as the snow became deeper the more we climbed. Suddenly we seemed to lose the path markers, and we were now wading through knee-deep snow that quickly became thigh-deep. The frustration of struggling against the heavy snow to make a few steps forward on an incline only to slip back further was intense. I had never felt the exhaustion of this kind before.

When this happened, lying down in that soft, deep snow was tempting. With the warm sun on my face, the wind seemed to whisper, 'take a rest'. So this was what it must feel like to give in to exhaustion in survival situations.

The voices of my brother and sister urging me to carry on seemed quite distant. I had to focus on getting my body upright again. My brother and sister took the lead so that father and I could step into their footprints which made life so much easier for us.

We were all grateful for Campino sweets. Strawberry and cream-flavoured shots of energy kept us going up that mountain – rationed and the reward for reaching the next natural marker like a rock or a bare branch of a lone tree.

We zigzagged our way up steadily, taking as direct a route as possible whilst avoiding what we could only assume was a ravine to the left of us by the way the snow draped across the landscape into a V shape. All lost in our thoughts of getting through this.

Reaching the neck of that mountain was a very high moment. The sun intermittently accompanied us up the mountain in between the grey clouds that bought bouts of gusty winds now stayed out as if to celebrate with us. That lovely, smooth expanse of untouched snow at the top glistened in the sunlight against the now brilliant blue sky.

In the distance, far ahead, tiny people moved up and down slopes. Gourette skiing resort. We whooped and smiled like never before. It didn't matter that there was still a last stretch descent into the village far below us.

I didn't care. We didn't care as long as we were heading down! We found ourselves sliding with joy down those snowy top slopes on the other side of that mountain. I don't recall how long it took us to make the descent. We were too happy. We had survived the ordeal.

The staff at the hostel in Gourette where we chose to spend the night did not believe us when we pointed to the four sets of tracks on the top slopes of the mountain that the sun was still illuminating, clearly visible from the veranda around which the twilight dusk was gathering.

We almost disbelieved it ourselves. Our drama under the skies in the South of France felt like it was so far away from the rest of the world, with just each other and the stunningly majestic landscape of the Pyrenees as witnesses.

In our room, we all sat down on the lower bunk beds and tried to absorb what we had been through. The essence of something bigger than us, guiding us forward and keeping us safe from harm, was profoundly and sacredly acknowledged.

The label on the bottle of red wine that accompanied our evening meal read 'Chemins de Pelerine', meaning 'Way of the Pilgrim'. Shall we go home now? We joked. It felt like we had done our Camino and hadn't set foot in Spain yet!

I learnt I was more capable, resilient and stronger than I had ever thought I could be – we all did that day. Looking back, I was surprised that despite this unexpected and dramatic experience on that day, it didn't drastically change the course of my life as one might think it would have. I didn't decide to become a nomad and give up the conventional life living from a rucksack or anything like that afterwards when I returned to a 'normal' life following the Camino.

Yet something had changed. Of course, it had. You don't go through an experience like that, and it doesn't change you on some level.

The outer challenge I had experienced was off the scale – particularly on that pass. The inner challenge of wrestling with my mindset that triggered the fear was far worse. Once you got over the physical obstacle of the environment, it was over. Yet the mind had its habit of creating worse things to anticipate, keeping my nervous system in a fight-or-flight state.

Looking back, it wasn't necessarily the height of the road that caused the fear itself. It wasn't necessarily the snow or the prospect of an avalanche occurring.

No, it was my thoughts causing the fear, the thoughts of slipping and falling but more painfully, something happening to my family up there. My thoughts held me hostage in those minutes before stepping out onto the stones and exposing myself to the landscape's vulnerability, the elements.

It was my thoughts pressing the reaction of the fear button.

I had to change my self-talk around these thoughts; I was forced to change it because if I didn't, I would have gone into a panic state. I had already experienced immobilising panic attacks, and I did not want one there. I had to focus on what I wanted – for us to get out of that situation safely.

The traumatic passage onto my first Camino was nothing short of a miracle; once the shock had settled and I was back entirely in my body and reflecting in quiet moments, I recalled with immense gratitude how the magic of the wind that had breathed a blizzard moments before we took tread on the road's edge but had held its breath to give us safe passage along it. If we had experienced the intense bursts of winds as we did at times on the mountain later, I do not think we could have safely walked that mountain pass. I recalled with gratitude how the sun shone on the col of the mountain for us and held back the menacing misty clouds that threatened to hide it.

I do not know how we found ourselves on that snowy mountain pass road high up in the Pyrenees that day, facing an impossible life experience. I was challenged to challenge my thoughts, beliefs and emotions that day.

If you are at a point in your life where you are feeling completely paralysed with anxiety about how to move forwards and wanting to turn back or are facing resistance about something in your life, take a look at your beliefs around the challenge. What are they telling you that you cannot do? Ask yourself, is this true?

Of course, there will be moments of paralysing resistance to a situation where there seems to be no going forward and no going back, and it will feel like you will be forever stuck in that painful emotional place. Know that your fears and anxieties are pointing you to look at your beliefs. That these emotions remind you to change your negative self-talk.

You have to trust that you are capable beyond your life challenges. Your legs may turn to jelly. Your stomach may churn. Your chest may feel frayed at the edges with fear. You may feel the dread of resistance. This is the body responding to your thoughts – to prepare you to fight or flight or freeze. Ask yourself, are those thoughts true? If the answer is no, change them to better serving thoughts. This is not a case of kidding yourself. Life responds to how you think and what you believe.

Non-serving beliefs are like the veil of grey, misty clouds threatening to take us off our path – the path to who we are and not what the voice has told us of our small beliefs. We are our path, and our feelings and beliefs either make it an enjoyable or a difficult path.

There are still times when I am about to fall asleep, if I allow my mind to think about what we did, I can still feel the remnants of panic in my chest. The body never forgets. I reassure that part of me when it does surface that I am safe; I survived and challenged my beliefs. I smashed through fear.

RITA PRESTON

RITAPRESTON.COM

Chapter 9

Stage Fright

By Rita Preston

I get stage fright, but I always say I'll gladly make a fool of myself for children, especially at Vacation Bible School (VBS). One afternoon while serving as Director, I spilled Mountain Dew™ on my shoes as I left the house.

I still did not know what tidbit I would tell the children to go with the day's Bible verse at Opening that evening. I dashed back and changed my shoes. I grabbed a pair of red tie-up flats with dozens of air holes for comfort on hot days, purchased in Austria during a university study trip in the 1980s. Those flats did not match my sundress, but they were quick and comfortable.

I arrived at church, flustered, still with no story. Teachers, volunteers, and the kids gathered in the sanctuary. I walked to the lectern, looking at those eager little faces and volunteers. I inhaled deeply. I walked away from the podium with a microphone in hand. Usually, I kept a death grip on the lectern while I spoke; the reason being two-fold: 1) I talk with my hands a lot, and holding on to the firm wood kept my waving hands curtailed and 2) No one could see the trembling in my hands if I held on tightly.

Walking away from the stand, gripping the mike tightly in one hand, I gestured with the other toward my red footwear. "What do these red shoes have to do with VBS tonight?"

I saw puzzled looks.

"Well, when I was a little girl, about the size of some of you, I went shopping with my mom, big sister, aunt, and cousin. They seemed grown-up; I was the only little kid. While the moms looked at clothes in one aisle, the cousins shopped in another.

Because I was so short, I could duck under the clothing racks, dashing back and forth between them. That was fun!

Then, suddenly, the moms weren't there!

I went back to the girls. They weren't there either! I was too short to see over the racks to find them!

In my mind, I could do only one thing, go to the front of the store and look. I didn't find them, but I watched the people. A man in a suit is no good. Teenagers, nope. I spotted a mom with kids, PERFECT. I ran to her and explained about my lost family. She understood and led me to the customer service desk. I could barely see the man above the counter. The manager sat me on the ledge and boldly spoke into the microphone, 'Would the mother of the little girl wearing red shoes please come to the front of the store?

I looked at my red sneakers, and they GREW right before me! They were huge! All I could see was red! BIG RED FEET!"

Mom appeared! She scooped me up, asking if I had gotten lost! I answered, 'No! You and the girls were lost!'

There were giggles from the crowd and knowing glances among the adults.

"What do those red shoes from long ago have to do with my red shoes tonight? I once was lost, but now I'm found, just like in the song *Amazing Grace*. My mom recognised me! These red shoes remind me that God knows how to find me when I get lost!"

Sometime during my storytelling, I realised how completely silent the sanctuary had become. The little ones were not fidgeting, unusual considering the hot summer evening in a big brick building with no air conditioning! My audience was silent as if hanging on my every word. I was overwhelmed.

Still, though, in the silence, my voice remained strong. I carefully walked across the chancel area so my red shoes remained fully visible to the crew. I could feel a warmth in my soul, unlike when I had been near fainting.

Without thinking, I took normal full breaths and savoured the words of the actual short story from my childhood.

The moments that followed were phenomenal. I felt aglow. The children beamed! My staff of almost 50 volunteers applauded.

When I dismissed them to their classrooms, several volunteers lingered briefly and gave me hugs. I was told that a miracle had happened that night. They had felt the impact of my story of being lost and found. I was humbled. There were tears.

I was thankful for divine inspiration, from spilt soda pop to choosing replacement shoes and finding words to a story I did not know was within me.

Several years later, one of my volunteers (a dear friend's mother) gave me a Christmas tree ornament: a beautiful red shoe.

Her daughter told me they had extensively searched for a red shoe ornament. Her mom never forgot the lost little girl with the red shoes who was found.

Sometimes we do not realise the lasting impact we have on the lives of others. Recognising our blessings, even if we are unaware that they are happening, is essential. We are doubly blessed if we are mindful of the impact. Hopefully, the effect is always positive and not negative!

Digressing to my college days, during which I took a quick one-month course in Austria to fit in some 'recommended' courses that my overfull semester schedules would not accommodate, I reflect on the many speeches I was required to deliver in various courses, from international studies to political science.

I had developed stage fright but didn't know the time frame. I knew only that for the few hours before class and presenting my speech, I would spend a considerable amount of time in the restroom, my body eliminating any nutrition I had attempted to devour. Before my speech, I took a glass of water, a cup of coffee or anything to keep my vocal cords wet. Nonetheless, I would walk to the podium, look out at my fellow students, glance at the professor, open my mouth, and feel as though I had just eaten enough cotton balls to play the lead role in the movie 'The Godfather'. Without fail, that was the speaking routine throughout my college years.

I supported the local pharmacy through my innumerable purchases of anti-diarrheal medications and antacids to settle my stomach. Nothing worked. Like clockwork, my trips to the bathroom started 2-3 hours before every scheduled speech.

Then, speech over, and class over, my stomach and system immediately returned to normal. No doctor could make sense of my crazy system; I had no virus and no stomach ulcers. In those days, anxiety was not a common diagnosis. I had stage fright, and who goes to the doctor for stage fright? Certainly not a twenty-something university student who wants to appear relaxed and professional!

The goal of the time was to make good impressions, acquire good recommendations, and move forward professionally.

Now in my late fifties, I look back and realise, many of us took our studies too seriously. I do not mean that we needed to join the ever-present party crowds, but rather that we took ourselves and the impact of our studies too seriously to be healthy.

133

Maybe not all of us, but I certainly did. I had a fantastic core group of friends, and it was common for us to max out our curriculum hours, adding extracurricular activities and church on Sundays. (The minimum credit hours for full-time status was 12; I took 18 every semester for all four years, even carrying 19 in one term. Let's hear it for loving a busy life!).

My parents permitted me a summer job during my college years, but I was not allowed to work part-time during the semesters. Mom assured me that my job was to get good grades. Neither Mom nor Dad ever reprimanded me if a grade was less than perfect. I pointed my declines, they nodded, and they assured me they knew I would pull them back up. At no time did they belittle me when I had struggles. I carried their ultimate faith on my shoulders. I had to do well in my mind. I would be the first to graduate from a four-year university.

The FEAR of public speaking continued and grew following commencement from university. Asked to speak at any gathering, and there was my physical nemesis, stomach upset, trembling hands, and cottonmouth.

During those busy college days, I attended an annual one-week missionary conference every summer. One of my favourite activities during that week was singing in the choir. I love to sing. Anyone who wanted to make a joyful noise at the conference was welcome. I found a voice with the choir, a strong, happy voice.

Did I ever sing a solo? I made sure to avoid solo work. Why? That went right along with my fear of public speaking. I was sure I would hit the wrong note; my voice might tremble, falling off the pitch and fading away. I was fearful I didn't have enough wind to sustain long notes.

Why was I afraid to appear alone on stage? I had no clue at the time. I love to sing! I have secretly beamed when someone tells me I have a beautiful voice.

My big sis has mentioned listening to my husband singing bass, our youngest son singing tenor, her singing alto, and me singing soprano in the back pew at church – and she loved the harmony. Of course, that was when we were younger and before our son went to military service.

I sing in the car with the radio, CDs, and sometimes acapella. I do not sing in the shower! I shied away from the church choir as an adult. But why? Did I shy away from speaking when asked?

No.

Why not?

I have always believed that when we are called upon to serve a need for others, especially in church, we must fulfil the call. As painful as it may be, we were not promised an easy life, but we are promised the strength for that which we must face.

One of our dearest friends is a pastor in the Evangelical Presbyterian Church. I was blessed to meet him during my first years as Vacation Bible School Director; he has inspired me. He left his nursing career to attend seminary and become a minister. His dear wife continued in the nursing field while he made the transition, and together, they raised three marvellous children.

In his final semester at seminary, my friend said, "I need a break. I need to take a semester off. I am burned out."

I almost snorted when I laughed. "My dear! You cannot take off a semester. You can see the light at the end of the tunnel. Statistics show that if you take off near the end of school, you never return! You cannot and will not quit! You know you cannot hide from God's plan for you!" The pastor smiled, took a deep breath, and said, "Oh, how well I know you cannot hide from His plan." Pastor finished seminary and has served several congregations over the years.

I was humbled again when I was asked to read a biblical passage at his ordination service. The passage states simply, "Here am I, Lord."

That passage sticks with me. Here I am. As I am called and led, so will I do, even when my stomach rumbles and my hands tremble to my fingertips.

Life is not always easy. Sometimes we end up on very different paths than we imagined when we were youngsters on a playground. Being open to adventure, accepting discomfort and change, and accepting things that frighten us all lead to adventure and life memories.

When we become 'elderly' and sit in a rocking chair, we need those memories to bring quiet smiles to our weathered faces.

In more recent years, someone mentioned school activities from the junior and senior high school eras during a moment of reminiscing. I played the clarinet, starting in 5th grade and joining the middle-school band by 7th grade. It was easy to get lost in a sea of woodwind instruments. I must confess; I loved the little competitions for 1st Chair and taking my turn in that seat.

I was signed up for chorus and band that first year in middle school. I was excited! I loved to sing! During the first week of classes, we had auditions within the group so that the choral Director could decide which parts to assign us. I had been told by the choir director at church that I had a fantastic range during youth choir, so he assigned me roles depending on who might be absent. I was thrilled!

The school choral director called us individually to sing back the notes he played on the old piano. I fell off a note. I fell flat. I heard laughter in the gallery from students I had not yet come to know (first year at the bigger combined school). I could feel the red glow up my neck, over my face, and into my ears. The Director played the notes again. My ears buzzed. I opened my mouth, and nothing musical escaped my vocal cords.

Within days, the chorus was removed from my schedule by the powers that be. I was humiliated.

I stayed with my trusted clarinet that I could make sing. I learned to play other versions of clarinets.

I kept my vocal cords silent. I made sure to excel in other academic pursuits. I no longer sang in my room at home with the old records on the player. Occasionally, notes escaped my lips, but I tended to listen more and sing less and less.

College arrived, and I had to present speeches.

In my first semester, I was assigned the course, Introduction to Speech. Horrors! I nailed it and earned bonus points on top of the A grade. I was terrified, and my instructor had no idea.

None of my instructors knew the physical toll those speaking requirements wore on my body. I made sure to excel no matter how miserable I felt.

Of all things, I was studying foreign languages.

I had a knack for learning languages and loved one-on-one conversations. I was in my realm with that talent and savoured meeting new people, anticipating a travel-related career, perhaps involving international relations. The world was going to be my stage, and I would fly!

But, oh, how miserable the path was at times.

When I sat for my oral comprehensive exams in front of three professors, I was nervous but not frightened. My stomach was fine. I admired the examiners and knew I could not feel foolish in front of them. Even knowing that that exam could prevent matriculation did not sway me. I enjoyed the assessment and passed.

Deep down, though, that ugly beast of fear was still there. I hid it well most of the time. I became good at conversing and known for talking a lot. Family members still point out that they cannot get a word in edgewise when I enter a conversation. I learned that if I chatter about any number of topics, I can effectively hide my fears, the things that might cause others to stare at me. If I can control the stage, I can control what is seen.

It has taken me years to learn what that fear is and that I do not have to hide it from anyone, including myself. Throughout my lifetime to date, there have been family worries, sicknesses, and grief. Speaking frankly with my family doctor (a.k.a. primary care physician) and, eventually, a private counsellor, I know I succumb to anxiety.

That is the name of the beast that reared its ugly head during that chorus tryout decades ago and tortured me ever since, telling me that someone will laugh at me when I am not good enough.

ANXIETY. Many experience anxiety in mild form throughout their lives, which is normal.

For some of us, it moves into our psyche and makes itself at home. Medical advice, diagnosis, and treatment are essential. Treatments range from self-help activities, personal journals, medication, and counselling.

There may be more, but that is for a professional to discuss. I am not a medical professional; I can only speak from personal experience and my journey to conquer what I thought was stage fright.

I am no longer afraid to speak in public.

I am incredibly self-conscious about singing in public and prefer to hear the notes to stay on key.

Eagerly, I sing with my grandchildren, and we laugh together, not at each other, if we hit the wrong notes.

I sing in my car, with the windows down, hoping the neighbours hear and laugh at the crazy lady singing too loudly.

When asked to speak in front of a group now, I accept and am honoured to do so. Sometimes my hands still tremble, but I know I have the floor. Anxiety is not the one who was asked to speak so that anxiety can step to the back row.

Divine inspiration comes when least expected, even from spilt soda. Breathe deeply and let the words flow. Fear disappears.

Epilogue

Thank you for purchasing a copy of this book. I hope you were able to find strength by reading the stories of others and sharing their experiences. If you are currently going through any of the experiences you've read within this book, please know that there is light at the end of the tunnel.

Look at the reflections from the Authors in here and try and find some answers for your own situation.

If you would like to share your own story, please do contact us for details on how you can take part in first becoming a Contributing Article Writer for our global magazine, MO2VATE and subsequently, Volume Two of this anthology.

If you enjoyed this book, we would love a review on Amazon.

Thank you again for taking the time to read our Authors' journeys.

Preview: Stories from around the Globe (Volume One) Women's edition

'Living Life on Purpose' by Olive Pellington

"When you know you were born for more than where you currently are and you know that you were put on this earth for a purpose, life begins to change. Somehow it seems like suddenly the sun just got a lot brighter. Truth be told, if we had been noticing the subtle changes, the slight nudges in course correction, we would have seen the beautiful morphing shades of the sunrise. But because we allow 'life' to get in the way, the nudges become shoves and the changes become cliff hangers. So, like any other insane entrepreneur, I decided to grow my wings on the way down. Thankfully, like an eagle, I don't stay down for long."

To purchase this book, click here:

https://amzn.to/2Rq1Jn8

Preview: Stories from around the Globe (Volume Two) Men's edition

"Little Girl Lost – On the Other Side' by Alison Wombwell

"July 2019 – the month and year that will forever stay with me. It was when my whole life changed. I had just received a diagnosis of Autism. I was Thirty-four years old.

At a time when I should have felt relieved and at peace finally understanding who I was, I did not. In fact, I felt incredibly low. I felt like everything that I thought I was, was a lie. It was like someone had said, you are autistic now, you can take your mask off, you can be yourself. I did not know how to be myself.

To purchase this book, click here:
https://amzn.to/34O6pq2

About the book creator

SHARON BROWN moved to the West Midlands in 2003 from Glasgow in Scotland. After a wide-ranging career in Event Management, Marketing, Project Management and board level support in various industries, Sharon started an Events Agency in 2015 which has grown into Lydian Group Ltd.

After realising that business was heading more towards the online digital space, Sharon launched four online platforms, the first being a Women in Business platform in 2018 with a mission of creating 'Collaboration over Competition'. Two further projects were launched during lockdown with the aim of helping small business owners build their brands through speaking, writing, publishing, and collaborative working. MO2VATE Magazine was born in 6 weeks from concept to implementation and received a fantastic following through its subscribers and supporters. It's now seeing a complete facelift this year ready for its relaunch as MO2VATE Media, seeing it evolve as a membership driven business and information hub.

The Speakers Index was the third platform to be launched as Sharon saw a gap in the market around Speaking Agencies and the lack of promotion towards their speakers. The Speakers Index is an online directory which also houses a quality Speakers Magazine highlighting the speakers' talents.

Members are encouraged to create a full profile giving all the information needed by an Organiser who can then contact them directly through their contact details on the website or in the magazine.

The Book Chief Publishing House is Sharon's latest project, launched in 2021, already with an impressive resume of clients and Authors. Sharon's vision was to provide an all-in-one affordable publishing service turning small business owners into credible authors through a robust and structured process. The Book Chief portfolio has exponentially grown during 2022 and continues to build huge momentum.

SERVICES

MO2VATE MEDIA

MO2VATE is a global digital business hub covering topics across business industries, health, inspiration, lifestyle, politics, opinion / research-based information, entrepreneur insights and many other topics, founded by Sharon Brown.

Formerly known as MO2VATE Magazine, this new platform launches in November 2022 with a completely new concept to share important information globally.

All articles are written by business owners and the project is managed by independent entrepreneurs. The online hub runs yearly International Awards and produces various books written by the Contributors who are part of the MO2VATE community.

Mo2vatemedia.com

editor@mo2vatemagazine.com

THE BOOK CHIEF PUBLISHING HOUSE

The Book Chief Publishing House was born during the latter end of the pandemic with a mission to support business owners on their path to becoming credible Authors.

The Book Chief publishes every genre, type and size of book and advises on every step of producing your book from book covers, titles, book descriptions, your best chance to become a best-selling Author and much more.

The Book Chief has a great track record in customer service and of producing great results for your book both in layout, editing, design and marketing.

As a one-stop shop for all your Publishing needs, and payment plans to spread the cost, it should be the first stop for those looking to publish and spread the word about their book!

Thebookchief.com

sharon@thebookchief.com

THE SPEAKERS INDEX

The Speakers Index is an online directory for speakers and event organisers designed to improve their chances of being seen by the right people.

We produce a quarterly magazine where each speaker features on a double page spread. The magazine is sent out through social media and to our email list on each publication.

Working similar to an agency but without any additional fees or commission, The Speakers Index also creates events to allow speakers to participate and be seen.

Thespeakersindex.com

sharon@thespeakersindex.com

Printed in Great Britain
by Amazon

12996825R10092